STOP
THE
WAR

A GRAPHIC
HISTORY

FOREWORD BY

TONY
BENN

Editorial Director ➤ Andrew Burgin
Editor ➤ Marie Gollentz
Design ➤ Péter Palásthy
Photography Research ➤ Guy Smallman
Art Research ➤ Ruth Boswell

The publication has been supported by the
Barry Amiel and Norman Melburn Trust

First published by Francis Boutle Publishers
and Stop The War Coalition

272 Alexandra Park Road
London N22 7BG
Tel/Fax: (020) 8889 7744
Email: info@francisboutle.co.uk
www.francisboutle.co.uk

Email: office@stopwar.org.uk
www.stopwar.org.uk

Printed and bound in Slovenia

ISBN 978 1 903427 59 0

TABLE OF CONTENTS

The Peace movement has always had powerful advocates over the years. But when after 9/11, Bush and Blair decided to invade Afghanistan, the Stop The War movement was founded and over the last ten years has been extremely influential. Stop The War drew support from across a wide political spectrum and organised literally hundreds of public meetings, up and down the country, to alert people to the dangers of that war and of the further dangers if a war against Iraq was launched as well.

In February 2003 just before the Iraq war began, two million people attended a massive demonstration in London warning of the death and destruction such a war would bring. This immediate campaign did not succeed in stopping that war but it built a structure of opposition which carried the day with the country so that when the Iraq attack was launched there was huge opposition.

The Government established the Chilcot Inquiry and when they report it is almost certain that they will declare the Iraq war to have been illegal. But whatever the outcome the Stop The War movement has turned out to be an excellent example of how public campaigns can be organised and how successful they can be. Those who worked to establish Stop The War and ran it so efficiently deserve a place in the modern legends of the Labour movement.

Tony Benn

Tony Benn
Stop The War President

❙❙ Guy Smallman
Don't Attack Iraq
15 February 2003

❙ James M. Thorne
Time to Go, Manchester
23 September 2006
Tony Benn

Ten years of the Stop The War Coalition cannot sensibly be a matter for rejoicing, since it means ten years of war as well. Much of what the Coalition predicted when Bush and Blair embarked on their 'war on terror' in the wake of 9/11 has come to pass. Indeed, the devastation wrought around the world has exceeded the most pessimistic prognoses of those days. Certainly, few of us anticipated in 2001 that the war would be continuing ten years later and with (conservative estimate) hundreds of thousands of dead.

The occupation of Afghanistan continues and, according to the occupiers, will do so for another four years at least. The war there has long since spread to and destabilised nuclear-armed Pakistan. The killing of Osama Bin Laden has resolved nothing. The death toll of British soldiers mounts, while more Afghan civilians are dying than ever. Terrorism has spread. Iraq lies in ruins, with millions displaced and hundreds of thousands killed as a consequence of what must rank as the bloodiest and most incompetent occupation ever, imposed in the aftermath of an entirely lawless and mendacious war.

David Cameron has proclaimed 'interventionism is back' after manoeuvring NATO, in concert with French President Sarkozy, into a war to change the regime in Libya to one more amenable to western interests. This mission, hypocritically sold as being about 'civilian protection', has led to many thousands of fatalities while it remains far from clear that it has bequeathed Libya a functioning administration. It is certainly not a sovereign one.

Given that, some may (and in fact do) ask what has the Stop The War Coalition achieved over the last decade? This book gives part of the answer – it illustrates the scope of the vast anti-war movement which developed from 2001, peaking in the demonstration of February 15th 2003. The diversity of that movement, both in terms of the people who supported it and the activities it undertook, is a remarkable fact of contemporary political life. Even if nothing had changed in terms of the course of events as a result, it would still have been a movement of immense importance, because it is through these activities that people themselves change, with enduring consequences.

However, it is wrong to assert that nothing changed as a result of the work of the Stop The War Coalition and its allies. Blair took this country into a catastrophic conflict against the wishes of most British people. His action was an outrage against democracy. His action has haunted him ever since and will follow him to his grave.

In the wake of the war, the Stop The War Coalition set itself three priorities – holding the government to account for its actions (Blair Out!); getting British troops out of Iraq, and preventing the extension of the war to other countries (Don't Attack Iran!). On all of these accounts the movement can record a measure of success – partial in some cases, belated in others, but nevertheless real. Other factors have been at work of course, not least the resistance of the people of Iraq to the occupation of their country. But our movement can be proud of the part it played in clipping the wings of war.

And plays. While the 'war on terror' continues, so does the work of the Coalition. It would be much happier to say that this book charts the movement from its beginning to its end. But the end is still ahead of us – in sight, but as yet unreached. This book should inspire us to redouble our efforts to reach that destination the sooner.

Andrew Murray

Deputy President of Stop The War
Chair of Stop The War 2001 – 2011

Lindsey German

Convenor of Stop The War

THE PEOPLE UNITED

From seasoned activists to first-time
marchers the truly extraordinary thing
about the Stop The War Coalition is its
breadth of support. Across the country
people of every age, race, culture and
religion came together in their millions
to send a message to Tony Blair and his
government: 'War Is Not The Answer'.

12

➤ Peter Marshall
Stop the War in Afghanistan
18 November 2001

❚ Paul Mattsson
No More Wars
20 March 2004

Peace Seen 020 8881 9386

Bliar
BLIAR!
Bliar.
Socialist Worker
BLAIR MUST GO!
UK/US troops out of Iraq

16

↑ Guy Smallman
Don't Attack Iraq
15 February 2003

↦ Guy Smallman
Don't Attack Iraq
15 February 2003

➤ Brian David Stevens
End the Occupation of Iraq
17 April 2004
George Galloway

❚ Paul Mattsson
Irish Anti-war Movement
25 June 2004
Dublin march

1 Guy Smallman
Peace Camp
16 March 2005
Trafalgar Square

↓ Geoffrey King
Peace Camp
18 March 2005
Trafalgar Square

↓ Guy Smallman
Don't Attack Iraq
15 February 2003
Critical Mass

23

→ Peter Marshall
End Israeli Occupation
18 May 2002
PSC demonstration

❙ Brian David Stevens
The Right to Protest
1 August 2005
Trafalgar Square

→ Guy Smallman
Gleneagles G8
5-6 July 2005

↑ Rudolf Cech
Blair at Chilcot Inquiry
29 January 2010

Bliar
Bliar
Bliar
Bliar
Iraq war lies illegality WMDs
spin folly credulity
shock and awe hubris
rogue states hypocrisy
collusion torture war on
Islamophobia body bags
failure rendition defeat
POLITAN
ICE

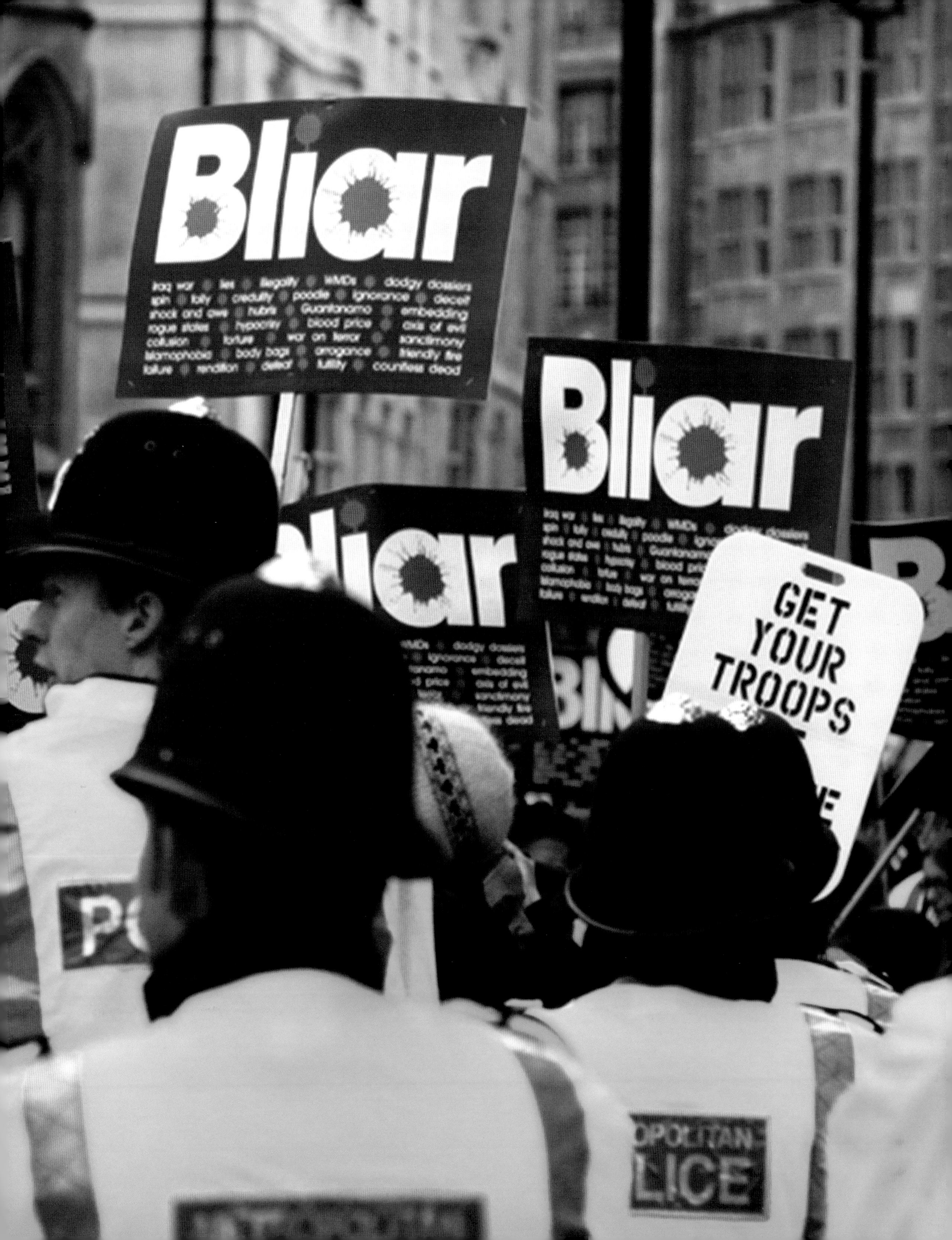
Bliar
Bliar
GET YOUR TROOPS

↑ Guy Smallman
The Right to Protest
1 August 2005
Brian Haw

← Guy Smallman
Bring the Troops Home
19 March 2005
Maxi Jazz

Guy Smallman
Don't Attack Iraq
15 February 2003
Hyde Park

39

→ Guy Smallman
Don't Attack Iraq
15 February 2003
Hyde Park

↑ Kristian Buus
Don't Attack Iraq
15 February 2003
Portraits in Hyde Park

Paul Mattsson
Opening Day of Parliament
8 October 2007
George Galloway and *Andrew Murray*

Paul Mattsson
Troops Home from Iraq
18 March 2006
Ken Livingstone

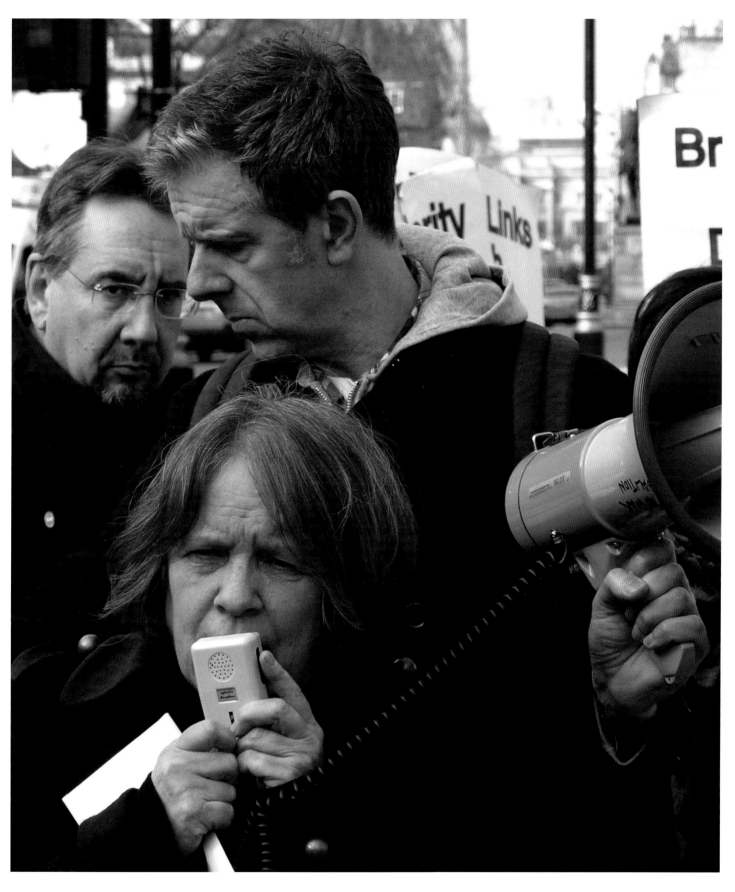

❚ Pete Riches
Stop the Bombing of Libya
12 March 2011
J. Rees, C. Nineham and *L. German*

❚ Richard Keith Wolff
London Guantánamo Campaign
23 November 2008
Abbey Road

❗ Marc Vallée
Bring the Troops Home
24 October 2009
Hetty Bower

⬆ Guy Smallman
Bring the Troops Home
19 March 2005
Martin Mubanga

⬇ Geoffrey King
Fifth Anniversary of Iraq Invasion
15 March 2008
Trafalgar Square

IN MEMORIAM

In an era of televised global conflict, we risk being desensitised to the horrors of war. Vigils organised for the dead reminded us of the shared despair of the deceased, from the families of British soldiers opposed to the war, to remembering those hundreds of thousands killed in the so-called 'war on terror'. The cost of war is more than the billions spent, it is a tragedy that should never be just expressed as a statistic.

← Paul Mattsson
Halloween Day of Action
31 October 2002

↑ Paul Mattsson
For Peace and Liberty
24 September 2005
Carla Hewett and *Susan Smith*

— Kristian Buus
Don't Attack Iraq
15 February 2003

DAUMA
0789 424 6104
6104

07586 531938
DAVID

DEAD

Stop the War Coa
DON'T
ATTACK
IRAQ

Mirror
Mirror

57

→ Paul Mattsson
Not in My Name
18 January 2003
Candlelit Vigil

↓ Paul Mattsson
Wreath Laying at Downing Street
10 November 2004
Rose Gentle

↓ Brian David Stevens
End the Occupation of Iraq
17 April 2004

60

➤ Brian David Stevens
Time to Go
20 November 2010

❘ Paul Mattsson
Stop the War
22 March 2003

FIGHTING BACK

We are often told passion has
disappeared from modern politics.
These images of protesters, young
and old, prove otherwise. Righteous
anger is an inevitable consequence
of injustice, and directed positively
it is a powerful and necessary tool.
Emotions are high because the stakes
are high too.

→ James M. Thorne
Lebanon: Ceasefire Now
5 August 2006

↑ Paul Mattsson
End the Occupation of Iraq
27 September 2003

68

↓ Guy Smallman
End Israel's Barbarism Now
22 July 2006

→ Guy Smallman
Day-X Students Strike
20 March 2003
Mass day of action

69

70

➥ Paul Mattsson
Day-X Students Strike
20 March 2003
Mass day of action

❙ Marc Vallée
Stop Gaza Massacre
10 January 2009

↑ Guy Smallman
End the Siege of Gaza
3 January 2009

← Guy Smallman
Stop Gaza Massacre
10 January 2009

↑ Guy Smallman
Stop Gaza Massacre
10 January 2009

CREATING PROTEST

The Stop The War Coalition has
proved time and again that protest
is not just about marching. The
theatrical and artistic skill on display
over the years has provoked both
thought and smiles. The techniques
and types of performance are legion,
but the underlying message is always
the same: the incredible creativity of
the people is one asset that can never
be privatised.

 Paul Mattsson
Faslane Blockade
4 July 2005

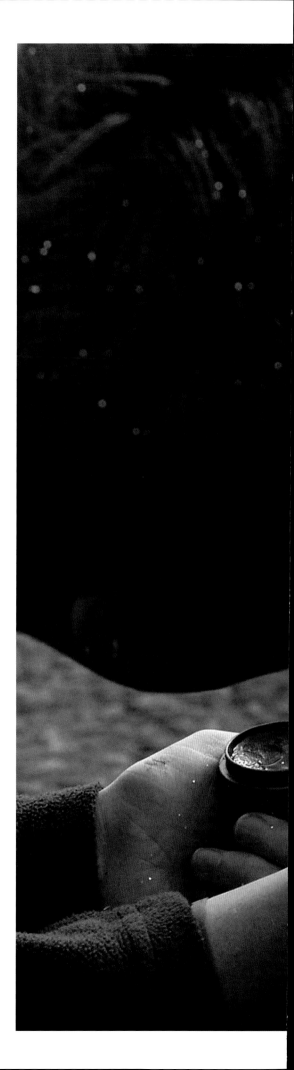

Paul Mattsson
Troops Home from Iraq
18 March 2006

↓ Guy Smallman
Bring the Troops Home
24 October 2009
Jonny 'Itch' Fox

↓ Guy Smallman
Bring the Troops Home
24 October 2009
Lowkey

↑ Guy Smallman
The Right to Protest
1 August 2005
Kate Hudson and *Pat Arrowsmith*

86

↓ Paul Mattsson
Faslane Blockade
4 July 2005

← Danelle Wessels
Time to Go
20 November 2010

↓ Peter Marshall
Troops Out of Iraq
22 May 2004

↑ Paul Mattsson
Troops Home from Iraq
18 March 2006

88

⚑ Brian David Stevens
The Right to Protest
1 August 2005

⚑ Brian David Stevens
End the Occupation of Iraq
27 November 2004

90

➤ Paul Mattsson
Shannon Airport
26 June 2004

→ Peter Marshall
Stop the War in Afghanistan
13 October 2001
CND demonstration

↓ Brian David Stevens
End the Occupation of Iraq
27 September 2003

Stop the War Coalition
DON'T ATTACK IRAQ
www.stopwar.org.uk

➥ Pete Riches
Stop Bush
20 November 2003

❘ Philip Wolmuth
Don't Attack Iraq
28 September 2002

98

➤ Brian David Stevens
Don't Attack Iraq
15 February 2003

← Paul Mattsson
End the Siege of Gaza
3 January 2009

↓ Paul Mattsson
Stop the War
8 March 2003
Manchester

Paul Mattsson
Don't Attack Iraq
28 September 2002

1 Guy Smallman
Stop Bush
20 November 2003

Paul Mattsson
Gleneagles G8
6 July 2005

Christian Payne
Don't Attack Iraq
15 February 2003

Philip Wolmuth
Peace and Justice for All
13 October 2001

THE ART OF POLITICS

The history of protest art is as rich
and long as that of protest itself.
The art supporting the anti-war
movement covers an extraordinary
range of styles, media and messages;
laugh-out-loud funny mingles with
the devastatingly poignant and
caustically satirical, from Steve Bell's
cartoons to David Gentleman's iconic
placards, from the photomontage
of Kennardphillipps to the street-art
of Banksy. This is the result of artists
standing up and saying:
'Not in My Name'.

Many of the images here are from
the Pax Britannica Exhibition that the
Aquarium Gallery produced for Stop
The War in 2004.

➥ Ralph Steadman
Guided Hard Copy
2003, London

110

↓ Ralph Steadman
War Kills
2003, London

← Ralph Steadman
Sheep on Cross
2004, London

112

➤ Martin Rowson
Wish We Weren't Here
2003, London

↕ Martin Rowson
Reclaiming the Streets
2002, London

➤ Martin Rowson
Not So Long After William Blake
2004, London

The war of Blair's Ear...

 Martin Rowson
Chilcot Inquiry
2009, London

➤ Martin Rowson
The War of Blair's Ear
2003, London

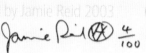

⊩ Jamie Reid
Peace Is Tough
2003, London

← Jamie Reid
The Evil Ones
2003, London

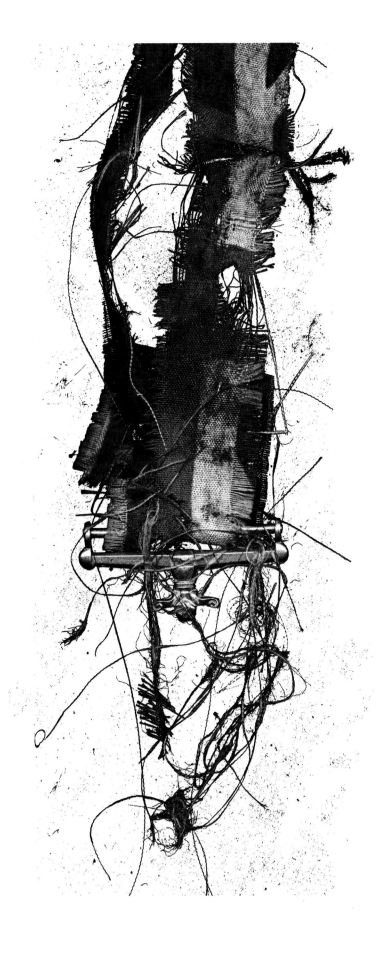

← Kennardphillipps
Peace on Earth
2003, London
Banned by Orange

↓ Kennardphillipps
Award#1
2004, London

↦ Peter Kennard
Union Mask
2003, London

↥ Kennardphillipps
The Mall
2005, London

↦ Kennardphillipps
Detail of Presidential Seal
2006, London

Printed by East End Offset Ltd (TU), London E3. ☎ 020 7538 2521

→ Kennardphillipps
Photo Op
2005, London

↑ Stop The War Coalition
B.liar
2003, London

IT IS BETTER TO JAW JAW THAN TO WAR WAR

WINSTON CHURCHILL

↓ Alan Kitching
It Is Better to Jaw Jaw Than to War War
2004, London

← Karmarama
Make Tea Not War
2003, London

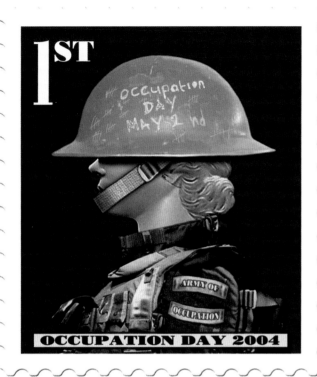

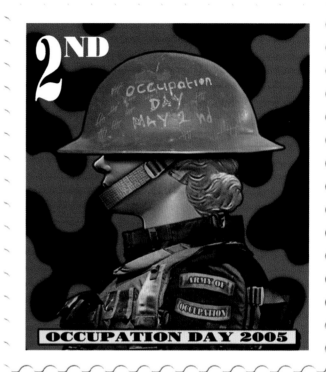

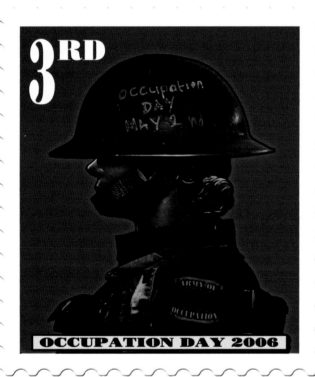

James Cauty
Stamps of Mass Destruction
2003-06, London

128

129

➥ Steve Bell
Cyclops Leaders
13 March 2003, London

↕ Steve Bell
Thanks to Jane Chatterjee
8 July 2003, London

➥ Steve Bell
Red Riding Hood
7 May 2003, London

130

grafica ROTELINE

TECHNICOLOR   TECHNISCOPE

IL BUONO
IL BRUTTO
IL CATTIVO

Le 7 sorelle del petrolio
presentano
COLIN POWELL & CONDOLEEZA RICE
TONY BLAIR   ARIEL SHARON   JOSÉ MARIA AZNAR
con la partecipazione straordinaria del **KUWAIT** e dell' **ARABIA SAUDITA**
con la collaborazione di **ABDULLAH GUL** (TURCHIA) e del **PAKISTAN**

NO WAR   una produzione **DONALD RUMSFIELD**

VERDI

BOLOGNA

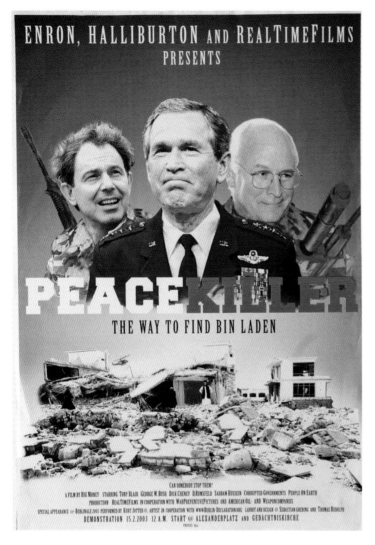

→ Verdi Bologna
Il Buono, Il Brutto, Il Cattivo
2003, Italy

↓ K. Jotter, S. Grering, T. Rudolph
Peace Killer
2003, Germany

↓ Comitato Fermiamo la guerra
Fermiamo la guerra all' Iraq
2003, Italy

'AS SOON AS THE FRENCH ARMY COMES IN SIGHT OF THE AUSTRIAN AND PRUSSIAN SOLDIERS THEY SHOULD INSTEAD OF ATTACKING THE ENEMY THROW DOWN THEIR OWN ARMS AND ADVANCE TOWARD THEM DANCING IN A FRIENDLY MANNER' ANACHARSIS CLOOTZ

133

→ Clifford Harper
Untitled
2003, London

↓ John Keane
Laser Guided
1991, London

James Boswell
Satirical Drawings
1943, London

136

NO
war on Iraq
axis of oil
brute force
friendly fire
body bags
blood price
collateral
smart bombs
orphans
imperialism
hypocrisy
heroics
quick fix
Stop the War Coalition www.stopwar.org.uk Poster number 3 by David Gentleman 2003

Stop the War Coalition www.stopwar.org.uk 020 7053 2153/4/5/6

Designed by David Gentleman Printed by East End Offset Ltd (TU), London E3. ☎ 020 7538 2521

→ David Gentleman
NO
2003, London

↑ David Gentleman
Bliar
2004, London

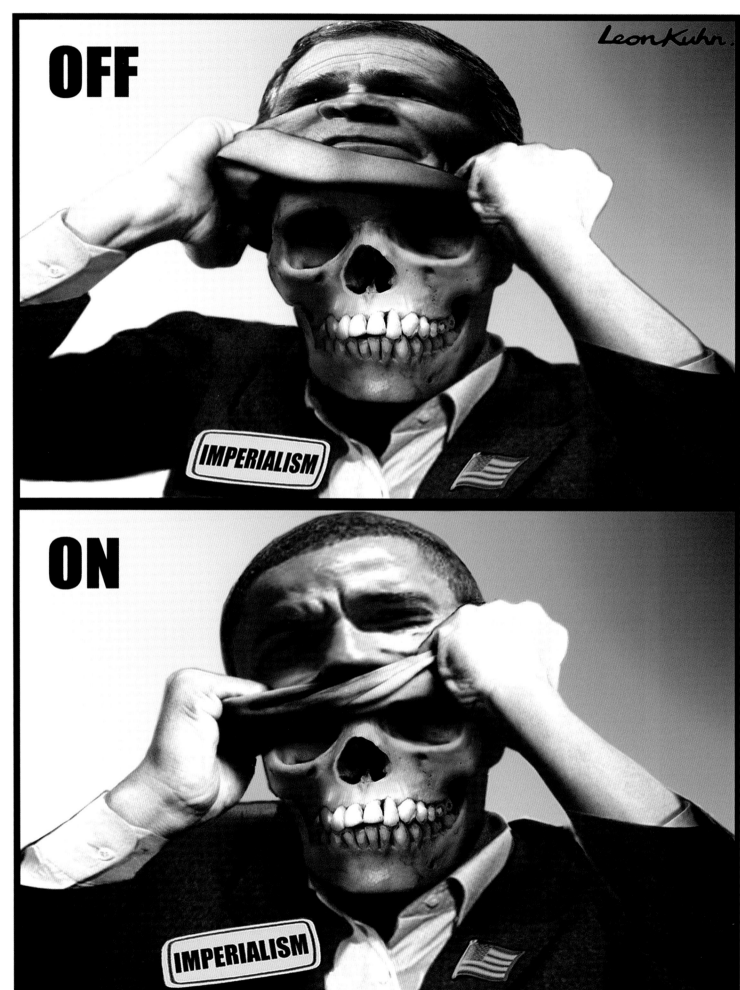

→ Leon Kuhn
Obama Unmasked
2008, London

↓ Leon Kuhn
US Parliament
2003, London

142

➥ Antonio Pacitti
Guantánamo Bay
2002, London

↓ Billy Childish
Soldier's Head With Hawk
2001, London

144

➡ Gee Vaucher
Still Life With Nude
2004, London

❗ Gee Vaucher
Welcome Home
2004, London

↓ Richard Hamilton
Installation Study, War Games
2004, London

← Richard Hamilton
Shock and Awe
2007, London

148

➜ Banksy
Wrong War
2004, London

↓ Banksy
Petrol Head
2005, London

STOP THE WAR:
A GRAPHIC TIMELINE

To the casual observer it is easy to get lost in the sheer magnitude of February 15th 2003, the largest day of international demonstrations in history – and perhaps understandably so. But the work started long before, and continues long after that one remarkable day. None of Stop The War's achievements would have been possible without the incredible work of committed local activists. A mass movement on this scale was built on an incessant timeline of action: conferences, concerts, peace camps, vigils, petitions, open letters, plays, concerts, club nights, blockades, public meetings, naming the dead ceremonies, talks, rock gigs, and, yes, demonstrations, across the United Kingdom and the world. Here are just some of them.

13 October 2001

Peace and Justice for All
CND demonstration

Sue Longbottom

18 November 2001

Stop the War in Afghanistan
Demonstration

Peter Marshall

---

21 September 2001

Founding Meeting of Stop The War
Friends Meeting House

---

13 October 2001

Peace and Justice for All
Campaign for Nuclear Disarmament demonstration

---

28 October 2001

Founding Conference of Stop The War

---

4 November 2001

Royal Court Theatre
Plays by *C. Churchill* and *T. Kushner*

---

18 November 2001

Stop the War in Afghanistan
Demonstration

---

24 January 2002

Guantánamo Bay
Protest at US Embassy

---

26 January 2002

Stop Israel's War on Palestine
Protest at Israeli Embassy

---

2 March 2002

Don't Attack Iraq
March to Trafalgar Square

---

4 March 2002

Don't Attack Iraq
Parliament rally

---

18 March 2002

Die-in
Parliament and Downing Street

26 January 2002

Stop Israel's War on Palestine
Protest at Israeli Embassy

2 March 2002

Don't Attack Iraq
March to Trafalgar Square

Peter Marshall

4 March 2002

Don't Attack Iraq
Parliament rally

Peter Marshall

18 March 2002

Die-in
Parliament and Downing Street

Guy Smallman

26 March 2002

Don't Attack Iraq
Rally

26 March 2002

Don't Attack Iraq
Rally

13 April 2002

Jenin Palestine Demonstration
Muslim Association of Britain

18 May 2002

End Israeli Occupation
Palestine Solidarity Campaign demonstration

8 June 2002

Not in My Name, Film
Rio Cinema

5 September 2002

Concert for Peace
F. Armstrong, L. Rosselson and *R. Johnson*

18 May 2002

End Israeli Occupation
PSC demonstration

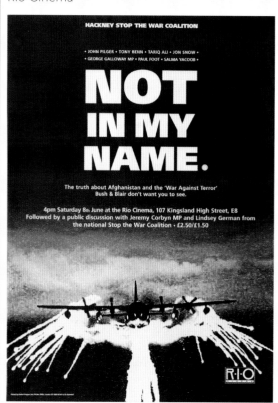

26-27

Peter Marshall

8 June 2002

Not in My Name, Film
Rio Cinema

Don't Attack Iraq
STW and MAB demonstration

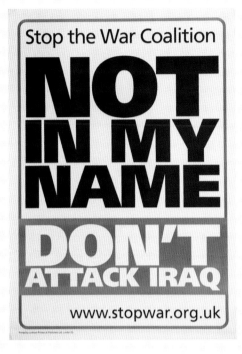

155

Louise Christian and *Jeremy Corbyn*
Peter Marshall

Don't Attack Iraq
STW and MAB demonstration

Bob Crow
Richard Searle

Guy Smallman

156

31 October 2002

Halloween Day of Action

Paul Mattsson

28 September 2002

Don't Attack Iraq
STW and MAB demonstration

31 October 2002

Halloween Day of Action

17-19 December 2002

First Cairo Conference

18 January 2003

Not in My Name
Candlelit Vigil

21 January 2003

STW Annual General Meeting
Camden Town Hall

14 February 2003

Make Love Not War

15 February 2003

Don't Attack Iraq
International demonstrations

5 March 2003

School Student Walkout

8 March 2003

Stop the War
Demonstration, Manchester

12 March 2003

The People's Assembly
Westminster Central Hall

18 January 2003

Not in My Name
Candlelit Vigil

Paul Mattsson

14 February 2003

Make Love Not War

Stop the War Coalition
MAKE LOVE NOT WAR
Valentine's Day, Friday 14 February
Eve of demonstration events

6pm Poets Against the War with **Michael Rosen**, **Linton Kwesi Johnson**, **Tony Harrison**, **Benjamin Zephaniah**, **Adrian Mitchell**, **Mr Social Control**, **Sarah Maguire**, **Mahmood Jamel**, **Moniza Alvi** and **Jean 'Binta' Breeze**. Bloomsbury Theatre, Gordon Street (Euston Square ⊖). £5 ☎ 020 7388 8822.

6.15pm The war on terror at home: how anti-terrorism affects migrant communities and refugees, with lawyer **Gareth Peirce**, **Dr Siddiqui** of the Muslim Parliament and author **Ghada Karmi**. Organised by the Campaign Against Criminalising Communities. Room 10/13, Friends Meeting House (Euston ⊖).

6.30pm Trade union rally with **Bob Crow** RMT, **Jack Heyman** president West Coast Longshoreman, **Mark Serwotka** PCS and **Billy Hayes** CWU, chaired by **Andrew Murray** Aslef. Bloomsbury Baptist Church, Shaftesbury Avenue, near junction with New Oxford Street (Tottenham Court Road ⊖).

6.30pm Globalise Resistance presents **Globalise This!** Video link-up with **Edward Said** answering your questions. Also live in London: **Daniel Correa** national coordinating committee MST landless movement, Brazil, **Soheir Morsy** Campaign to Confront US Aggression, Egypt, **Antonino Campenni** Cobas and arrested Social Forum activist, Italy. Hong Kong Lecture Theatre, Clement Building, London School of Economics, Aldwych (Temple/Holborn ⊖).

6.40pm Stop the War Coalition special movie opening: Alex Cox introduces his new film **Revengers Tragedy**, starring Christopher Eccleston, Derek Jacobi, Sophie Dahl and Eddie Izzard. Curzon cinema, Shaftesbury Avenue (Leicester Square ⊖). £8 ☎ 020 7734 2255.

7.30pm Stop the War Coalition rally: don't attack Iraq, with **Tony Benn**, **Ahmed Ben Bella**, **Yvonne Ridley**, **Bianca Jagger**, **Denis Halliday** and **John Rees**. Friends Meeting House, Euston Road (Euston ⊖).

8.30pm Ken Loach and Stephen Frears introduce **11.09.01** and **Dirty Pretty Things**. Bloomsbury Theatre, Gordon Street. (Euston Square ⊖). £10 ☎ 020 7388 8822.

Cafe Bookmarks special late opening minutes walk from the events of the evening of 14 February. Drop in for anti-war books and refresh yourself with a coffee, tea and cake plus an exhibition of anti-war images from artists including **Peter Kennard** and **David Gentleman**. Bookmarks open from 10am, cafe from 5pm till 10pm, 1 Bloomsbury Street (Tottenham Court Road ⊖).

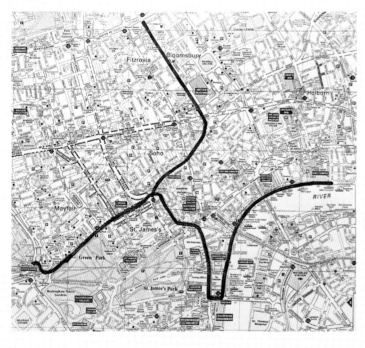

The official demonstration route

Don't Attack Iraq
International demonstrations

Tony Benn and *Jesse Jackson*
Guy Smallman

Tim Robbins
Guy Smallman

NO

war on Iraq
axis of oil
brute force
friendly fire
body bags
blood price
collateral
smart bombs
orphans
imperialism
hypocrisy
heroics
quick fix

Stop the War Coalition www.stopwar.org.uk Poster number 3 by David Gentleman 2003

Design: David Gentleman

159

Don't Attack Iraq
International demonstrations

8 March 2003

Stop the War
Demonstration, Manchester

12 March 2003

The People's Assembly

15 March 2003

One Big No Concert
Shepherd's Bush Empire

18 March 2003

Lobby of Parliament

Paul Mattsson

Day-X Students Strike
Mass day of action

School student activists' forum

If you're a school student and you're against the war, come along to discuss how our action can help to stop it, and how we can organise in our schools against it. Come and elect students to represent school groups from across the country. *This forum is run and organised by school students!*

Sunday 16 March 2003
Small Hall, Friends Meeting House,
Euston Road, London
Nearest ⊖ Euston (Victoria and Northern Lines)
Starts 11am

For more information please ring Hannah on 07984 205 125
or Leoni on 07946 843 745, or e-mail
school_students_stw_forum@hotmail.com

All school and sixth form students welcome
Printed by United Posters Ltd, PO Box 6381, London E3 3NB ● Not to be flyposted

162

Tariq Ali
Guy Smallman

Guy Smallman

Student Day of Action Against War 19th March

-Blair is spending billions on an unjust war on iraq while students in this country face the introduction of top-up fees.

-This war is not in our name and we will not study in these circumstances.

Walk out!
Protest 11.00 outside
The Houses of Parliament

5th March, school students walk-out against the war.

Call 0781 790 913 /
email studentstopwar@yahoo.co/uk for more detai

22 March 2003

Stop the War
Demonstration

Stop the War Coalition www.stopwar.org.uk 020 7053 2153/4/5/6

58-59

15 March 2003

One Big No Concert
Shepherd's Bush Empire

18 March 2003

Lobby of Parliament

19 March 2003

Student Day of Action Against War

20 March 2003

Day-X Students Strike
Mass day of action

22 March 2003

Stop the War
Demonstration

29 March 2003

Stop the War
Regional demonstrations

12 April 2003

End the Occupation of Iraq
Demonstration

28 August 2003

Hutton Inquiry
Picket

27 September 2003

End the Occupation of Iraq
Demonstration

24 October 2003

Defend George Galloway
Protest

12 April 2003

End the Occupation of Iraq
Demonstration

27 September 2003

End the Occupation of Iraq
Demonstration

Brian David Stevens

Stop Bush
Demonstration

Ron Kovic
Paul Mattsson

17 January 2004

The Hijab
A woman's right to choose

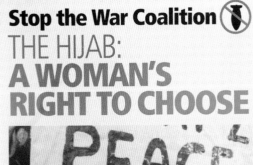

20 November 2003

Stop Bush
Demonstration

17 January 2004

The Hijab
A woman's right to choose

28 January 2004

Hutton Inquiry Report
Parliament Square protest

31 January 2004

No to the Hutton Whitewash
Downing Street protest

16 March– 17 April 2004

Pax Britannica – A Hellish Peace
Art exhibition at the Aquarium Gallery

20 March 2004

No More Wars
Demonstration

17 April 2004

End the Occupation of Iraq
Demonstration

22 May 2004

Troops Out of Iraq
Demonstration

25 June 2004

Irish Anti-war Movement
Dublin march

26 June 2004

Shannon Airport
Protest at US military base

20 March 2004

No More Wars
Demonstration

16 March– 17 April 2004

Pax Britannica – A Hellish Peace
Art exhibition at the Aquarium Gallery

Design: Ralph Steadman

17 April 2004

End the Occupation of Iraq
Demonstration

Brian David Stevens

22 May 2004

Troops Out of Iraq
Demonstration

Andrew Murray and *Yvonne Ridley*
Peter Marshall

25 June 2004

Irish Anti-war Movement
Dublin march

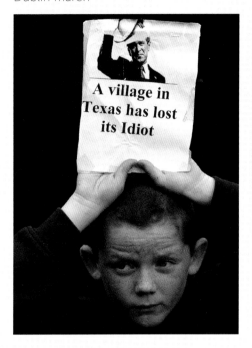

Paul Mattsson

Paul Mattsson

26 June 2004

Shannon Airport
Protest at US military base

Paul Mattsson

19 August 2004

Maxine Gentle Letter to Tony Blair
MFAW

'THIS WAR IS WRONG'

Messages from military families

From Reg Keys

Father of Lcpl Tom Keys, Royal Military Police, killed 24th June 2003 Iraq

I would like to voice my support to the brave personnel currently involved in operations in Iraq who are dedicated to doing their duty.

I feel that the most effective way of showing my support is to influence a prompt safe return with the respect and dignity they so rightly deserve...

'WE WON'T FIGHT THIS WAR'

Messages from British soldiers

From Ray Hewitt

1991 Gulf War veteran and Desert Rat

I joined the army when I was 16, and after completing basic training I returned to my school as a 'Satisfied Soldier' where I urged others to enlist.

My illusions of war being glorious were shattered in 1991 as I stood in the killing fields of Iraq. The true horror of war is difficult to describe. Every day our artillery would pound the Iraq positions with high explosive shells while our planes dropped napalm and cluster bombs on them...

17 October 2004

European Social Forum
Anti-war demonstration

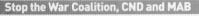

Stop the War Coalition, CND and MAB

Join the international demo organised
by the European Social Forum

TIME TO GO
BUSH OUT
TROOPS OUT

DEMONSTRATE
Sunday 17 October, 1pm,
Russell Square, London WC1
for march to Trafalgar Square
(nearest tubes Euston, Russell Square and Holborn)

www.stopwar.org.uk
020 7278 6694

Duncan Brown

TERRORISTES !

RETRAIT DES
TROUPES D'IRAK !

PAS DE PARTICIPATION
FRANCAISE !

Agir Contre la Guerre (ACG)

agircontrelaguerre@yahoo.fr   01 42 62 24 45
http://agircontrelaguerre.free.fr   06 16 42 27 87

1 November 2004

Moscow Piano Trio Concert

CONCERT FOR THE CHILDREN OF IRAQ

Monday 1 November 2004
7.30pm
Hackney Empire
291 Mare Street
London E8 1EJ

Concert in aid of the charity
Child Victims Of War

The Medici Quartet Mozart
quartet in G major & Ravel quartet
The Moscow Piano Trio Dmitry
Shostakovich: Passacaglia &
finale from the trio no 2 op.67
in E minor
Mohydeen Quandour World
premiere of trio 'Cry Jerusalem'
Mayor of London Ken
Livingstone Opens the concert
Plus **Jenny Matthews** Recent

Booking
To book tickets contact the
Hackney Empire box office
020 8985 2424 or
www.hackneyempire.co.uk

Prices
£10–£50 Champagne boxes at
£150 for four people

Further information

4 November 2004

Poets for Peace
Conway Hall

POETS FOR PEACE

featuring

Jean Binta Breeze
Terry Jones
Christopher Logue
Adrian Mitchell
Brian Patten
Michele Roberts
and introduced by Jonathan Pryce
Thursday November 4th 2004 7.30pm
Conway Hall Red Lion Square WC2
TICKETS £11 includes glass of wine
tel:020 7734 8932 or email:yarns@rippingyarns.co.uk

7 days for IRAQ
STOP THE WAR

10 November 2004

Wreath Laying at Downing Street
MFAW

Reg Keys
Paul Mattsson

27 November 2004

End the Occupation of Iraq
Demonstration

17 December 2004

Christmas Benefit Concert

BENEFIT CONCERT
Medical Aid for Iraq & Stop the War Coalition

Compere John Hegley

Alex Valentine
Bob Davenport
Carol Grimes
Celloman Ivan Hussey
John Hegley
Robb Johnson
The Angel Band

St.James's Church 197 Piccadilly
Friday 17 December 7.30pm

To book tickets or send donations
Call 020 7278 6694 Tickets £10 & £8

Nearest Tube: Piccadilly & Green Park

Peace is not just for Christmas

19 August 2004

Maxine Gentle Letter to Tony Blair
MFAW

10 November 2004

Wreath Laying at Downing Street
MFAW

17 October 2004

European Social Forum
Anti-war demonstration

27 November 2004

End the Occupation of Iraq
Demonstration

1 November 2004

Moscow Piano Trio Concert

17 December 2004

Christmas Benefit Concert

2 November 2004

Naming of the Dead
Trafalgar Square

21 January 2005

Counter Inauguration for G. W. Bush
Outside the US Embassy

4 November 2004

Poets for Peace
Conway Hall

16-18 March 2005

Peace Camp
Trafalgar Square

16-18 March 2005

Peace Camp
Trafalgar Square

Judy Linehan
Guy Smallman

Bring the Troops Home
Demonstration

Design: Billy Childish

Jamal Elshayyal
Guy Smallman

Guy Smallman

Bring the Troops Home
Demonstration

George Solornou
Peter Marshall

30 April 2005

Muslims United Against Oppression
Demonstration

Christian Payne

19 March 2005

Bring the Troops Home
Demonstration

30 April 2005

Muslims United Against Oppression
Demonstration

2 July 2005

Make Poverty History
Edinburgh

3 July 2005

Naming of the Dead
Monument on Calton Hill, Edinburgh

4 July 2005

Faslane Blockade

2 July 2005

Make Poverty History
Edinburgh

Paul Mattsson

3 July 2005

Naming of the Dead
Monument on Calton Hill, Edinburgh

Guy Smallman

4 July 2005

Faslane Blockade

Paul Mattsson

5-6 July 2005

Gleneagles G8
Demonstration

Guy Smallman

17 July 2005

Vigil for the Victims of 7/7
Russell Square

Paul Mattsson

5-6 July 2005

Gleneagles G8
Demonstration

9 July 2005

Vigil for the Victims of 7/7
Peace Gardens – Friends Meeting House

17 July 2005

Vigil for the Victims of 7/7
Russell Square

1 August 2005

The Right to Protest
Parliament Square

15 September 2005

Letter at Downing Street

1 August 2005

The Right to Protest
Parliament Square

Brian David Stevens

Letter at Downing Street

Brian Eno and *Julie Christie*
Guy Smallman

For Peace and Liberty
Demonstration

Design: Jamie Reid and the Aquarium

Military Families with *Bianca Jagger*
Paul Mattsson

Brian David Stevens

For Peace and Liberty
Demonstration

Guy Smallman

Brian David Stevens

18-19 October 2005 ►

MFAW Peace Camp
Downing Street

Rose Gentle, Jeremy Corbyn, Helen Brierley, Phil Shiner and *Peter Brierley*
Guy Smallman

18-19 October 2005

MFAW Peace Camp
Downing Street

Kristian Buus

27 November 2005

Rachid Taha Band
Astoria Concert

Rachid Taha
and *Brian Eno*

24 September 2005

For Peace and Liberty
Demonstration

18-19 October 2005

MFAW Peace Camp
Downing Street

27 November 2005

Rachid Taha Astoria Concert
With *Brian Eno, Imogen Heap* and *Nitin Sawhney*

10 December 2005

International Peace Conference
London

31 January 2006

Naming of the Dead
100th British soldier killed in Iraq

18 March 2006

Troops Home from Iraq
Demonstration

30-31 March 2006

Condoleezza Not Welcome Here
Liverpool and Blackburn

4 April 2006

Banksy Installation
Brian Haw Peace Camp

26 April 2006

Naming of the Dead
MFAW

10 June 2006

Fifth Annual STW Conference
Friends Meeting House

10 December 2005

International Peace Conference
London

Cindy Sheehan

Peter Brierley

Tony Benn

Jawad al-Khalisi

Elaheh Koolaee

Sami Ramadani

31 January 2006

Naming of the Dead
100th British soldier killed in Iraq

Dario Fo

Kate Hudson

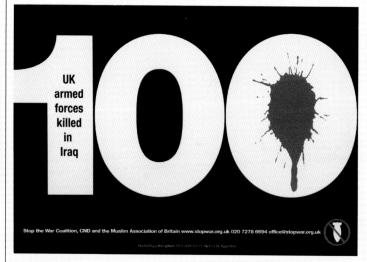

Photographs: Guy Smallman

18 March 2006

Troops Home from Iraq
Demonstration

180

Installation: David Gentleman
Paul Mattsson

Installation: David Gentleman
Paul Mattsson

Guy Smallman

30-31 March 2006

Condoleezza Not Welcome Here
Liverpool and Blackburn

4 April 2006

Banksy Installation
Brian Haw Peace Camp

Richard Keith Wolff

26 April 2006

Naming of the Dead
MFAW

Rose Gentle
Duncan Brown

18 July 2006 ➤

Vigil for Lebanon
Parliament Square

Guy Smallman

← 18 July 2006

Vigil for Lebanon
Parliament Square

Guy Smallman

Guy Smallman

182

22 July 2006

End Israel's Barbarism Now
Against Israeli bombing of Lebanon

Guy Smallman

Lebanon: Ceasefire Now
Demonstration

Labour Party Conference
Demonstration, Manchester

183

Picture: Ray Smith

John Tester

Labour Party Conference
Demonstration, Manchester

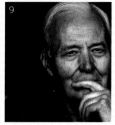

Leon Kuhn: Mad dogs and Englishmen
John Tester

184

11 November 2006

MFAW Naming of the Dead
Cenotaph, Whitehall

Peter Marshall

18 February 2007

Press Conference
No Trident demonstration

Guy Smallman

24 February 2007

No to Trident, Troops Out of Iraq
Demonstration

Roy St Pierre

Chris Blake

Guy Smallman

14 March 2007

No Trident Rally

Peter Marshall

24 May 2007

Troops Out of Our Schools
Public meeting

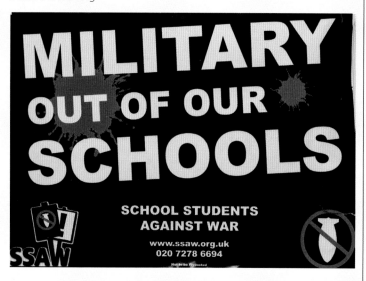

8 October 2007

Opening Day of Parliament
Demonstration

28 June 2006

A Night of Conscience
For Flight Lieutenant Malcolm Kendall-Smith

18 July 2006

Vigil for Lebanon
Parliament Square

22 July 2006

End Israel's Barbarism Now
Against Israeli bombing of Lebanon

28 July 2006

Lebanon: Ceasefire Now
Demonstration, Downing Street

5 August 2006

Lebanon: Ceasefire Now
Demonstration

11 August 2006

Unconditional Ceasefire Now
Demonstration, Downing Street

23 September 2006

Labour Party Conference
Demonstration, Manchester

11 November 2006

MFAW Naming of the Dead
Cenotaph, Whitehall

18 November 2006

The People's Assembly

24 January 2007

Debate on Iraq at Parliament
Demonstration outside Westminster

World Against War
International Peace Conference

Ibrahim Moussawi

Marzieh Mortazi Langroudi

Hassan Jumaa

Dennis Halliday

Hans von Sponeck

Daud Abdullah

Hamdeen Sabahy

George Martin

John Rees

Muna Coobtee

Photographs: Guy Smallman

15 February 2007

Protest at Blair's Visit
Glasgow

18 February 2007

Press Conference
No Trident demonstration

21 February 2007

No Trident Replacement
CND projection onto Parliament

24 February 2007

No to Trident, Troops Out of Iraq
Demonstration

14 March 2007

No Trident Rally

20 March 2007

The People's Assembly
Central Hall

24 May 2007

Troops Out of Our Schools
Public meeting

4 June 2007

STW Benefit at the Scala
Tom Morello, *Ed Harcourt*, *Frank Turner* and *Mark Steel*

28 June 2007

Blair's Last Day
MFAW protest at Downing Street

8 October 2007

Opening Day of Parliament
Demonstration

27 January 2008

End the Siege of Gaza

15 February 2008

Fifth Anniversary of February 15
Downing Street

Guy Smallman   Guy Smallman

Lindsey German, *Walter Wolfgang*, *Anas Altikriti*, *Tony Benn*, *Andrew Murray*, *Jeremy Corbyn*, *Kate Hudson*, *David Gentleman*, *Bianca Jagger*, *Louise Christian* and *Hetty Bower*
Guy Smallman

15 March 2008

Fifth Anniversary of Iraq Invasion
Demonstration

Mark Liebenberg

48-49   Paul Mattsson

Andrew Burgin
Geoffrey King

3 April 2008

The Wall of Sound
Westminster Cathedral

Richard Keith Wolff

15 June 2008

Bush Not Welcome Here
State visit of G. W. Bush

Guy Smallman

Guy Smallman

28 August 2008

Hand-in to Downing Street

*Kate Hudson, Brian Eno, Chris Nineham, Tony Benn,
David Gentleman* and *Lindsey German*
Guy Smallman

20 September 2008

Labour Party Conference
Demonstration, Manchester

Paul Mattsson

23 November 2008

London Guantánamo Campaign
Abbey Road

28 December 2008

Stop Bombing Gaza

Ismail Patel and *George Galloway*
Guy Smallman

30 November 2007

Rhythms for Peace
St James' concert

1 December 2007

World Against War
International Peace Conference

27 January 2008

End the Siege of Gaza

15 February 2008

Fifth Anniversary of February 15
Downing Street

15 March 2008

Fifth Anniversary of Iraq Invasion
Demonstration

3 April 2008

The Wall of Sound
Westminster Cathedral

24 April 2008

Illuminations: Concert for Peace
St James' concert

15 June 2008

Bush Not Welcome Here
State visit of G. W. Bush

28 August 2008

Hand-in to Downing Street

20 September 2008

Labour Party Conference
Demonstration, Manchester

3 January 2009

End the Siege of Gaza
Demonstration

10 January 2009 ➤

Stop Gaza Massacre
Demonstration

Guy Smallman

Marc Vallée

— 10 January 2009

Stop Gaza Massacre
Demonstration

Peter Marshall

17 January 2009

End the Siege of Gaza
Demonstration

John Tester

3-4 April 2009

No to NATO
Strasbourg

21 May 2009

Two Plays for Gaza
Hackney Empire

A Barebones Production to raise funds for
the Gaza Music School + Stop the War Coalition

Seven Jewish Children
by Caryl Churchill
+
The Trainer by David
Wilson + Anne Aylor

Staged readings directed by Tom Platten,
performed by Tim Pigott-Smith, Corin
Redgrave, Janie Dee, Jana Zeineddine,
Kika Markham, Roger Lloyd Pack + others

Plus music + song by Reem Kelani,
percussion by Eugene Skeef + words
by Tony Benn

To find out more about Stop the War Coalition and the
Gaza Music School, please visit www.stopwar.org.uk
or email david@stopwar.org.uk

"What [Churchill] captures, in…condensed
poetic form, is the transition that has overtaken
Israel, to the point where security has become
the pretext for indiscriminate slaughter."
—**Michael Billington**, *The Guardian*

"David Wilson and Anne Aylor's play makes a
surreal case for less government interference in
our lives and an emotional plea for peace, love
and understanding." —**Tim Pigott-Smith**

"The Trainer takes the scandal of an artist
bankrupted by the state – the composer Keith
Burstein – and brilliantly exposes the threat to our
freedoms and civil liberties." —**Corin Redgrave**

Two plays for **Gaza**

7.30pm Thursday 21st May 2009
Hackney Empire
291 Mare Street London E8 1EJ

For tickets (£15)
call the Hackney Empire box office on
020 8985 2424 or
visit www.hackneyempire.co.uk

23 November 2008

London Guantánamo Campaign
Abbey Road

28 December 2008

Stop Bombing Gaza

30 December 2008

Stop Bombing Gaza

January 2009

Gaza – Student Occupations

3 January 2009

End the Siege of Gaza
Demonstration

10 January 2009

Stop Gaza Massacre
Demonstration

17 January 2009

End the Siege of Gaza
Demonstration

24 January 2009

Gaza Protest outside BBC

14 February 2009

Valentine's Day Aid Convoy
For Gaza

1-2 April 2009

G20 Protests
ExCel Centre

23 July 2009

Rally at Conway Hall

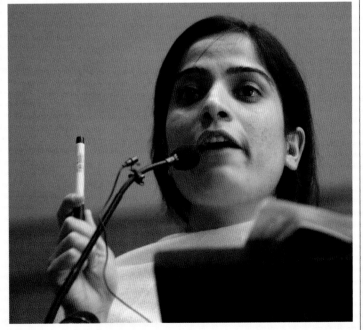

Malalai Joya
Guy Smallman

17 August 2009

Naming of the Dead
Cenotaph, Whitehall

Guy Smallman

23 October 2009

Stop the War, Start the Music
Beats Beat Bullets

Bring the Troops Home
Demonstration

Kika Markham and *Corin Redgrave*
Richard Keith Wolff

Joe and *Clare Glenton*
Marc Vallée

← 24 October 2009

Bring the Troops Home
Demonstration

Rudolf Cech

27 December 2009

Remember Gaza

Marc Vallée

3-4 April 2009

No to NATO
Strasbourg

---

16 May 2009

Remember Gaza
Demonstration

---

21 May 2009

Two Plays for Gaza
Hackney Empire

---

24 June 2009

Protest Outside Parliament
Calling for an open public Iraq Inquiry

---

23 July 2009

Rally at Conway Hall

30-31 July 2009

Chilcot Inquiry

---

17 August 2009

Naming of the Dead
Cenotaph, Whitehall

---

23 October 2009

Stop the War, Start the Music
Beats Beat Bullets

---

24 October 2009

Bring the Troops Home
Demonstration

---

12 November 2009

Free Joe Glenton
Ministry of Defence

29 January 2010

Blair at Chilcot Inquiry
Protest

Guy Smallman

5 March 2010

Joe Glenton Jailed

5 June 2010

Stop Islamophobia
Conference

Ken Loach

Caroline Lucas

Salma Yaqoob

Photographs: Danelle Wessels

Guy Smallman

6 December 2009

Viva Palestina Aid Convoy

27 December 2009

Remember Gaza

28 January 2010

Blockade London Afghan Conference

29 January 2010

Blair at Chilcot Inquiry
Protest

5 March 2010

Joe Glenton Jailed

26 July 2010

Afghanistan Time to Go
Rally

20 November 2010

Time to Go
Demonstration

Brian David Stevens

Guy Smallman

60-61

87

21 April 2010

Free Joe Glenton
Protest

12 July 2010

Joe Glenton Released
Colchester

31 May 2010

Protest Attack on Mavi Marmara

26 July 2010

Afghanistan Time to Go
Rally

5 June 2010

Stop Islamophobia
Conference

16 November 2010

Stop the War in Afghanistan and Pakistan
Public meeting

22 June 2010

Budget Day Protest
Parliament Square

20 November 2010

Time to Go
Demonstration

28 June 2010

Cut the War, Scrap Trident
Meeting in Parliament

21 January 2011

Blair at Chilcot Inquiry
Protest

21 January 2011

Blair at Chilcot Inquiry
Protest

Cat Phillipps and *Peter Kennard*
Jenny Matthews

Bruce Kent
Pete Riches

29 January 2011

Solidarity with Egypt
Demonstration

12 February 2011

Global Day of Action for Egypt
Amnesty – TUC Rally

Pete Riches

6 February 2011

Lois Atherden
Bristol Peace Vigil

Cliff Hanley

22 February 2011

Middle East Solidarity
Demonstration

Safa Kadhim

25 February 2011

Middle East Solidarity
Demonstration

Shamiul Joarder
Pete Riches

12 March 2011

Stop the Bombing of Libya
Downing Street

Chris Nineham
Pete Riches

29 January 2011

Solidarity with Egypt
Demonstration

6 February 2011

Lois Atherden
Bristol Peace Vigil

12 February 2011

Global Day of Action for Egypt
Amnesty – TUC Rally

22 February 2011

Middle East Solidarity
Demonstration

25 February 2011

Middle East Solidarity
Demonstration

12 March 2011

Stop the Bombing of Libya
Downing Street

16 May 2011

Stop the Bombing of Libya
Downing Street

21 May 2011

Confronting Islamophobia
Conference

24 May 2011

Stop the Obama Wars
Buckingham Palace

11 June 2011

Afghanistan and the War on Terror
Conference

ACKNOWLEDGEMENTS

First, our thanks go to all the photographers and artists who have allowed their work to be used free of charge. They have been a vital part of the work of the Stop The War Coalition over the last ten years. We owe a particular debt of gratitude to David Gentleman who provided the art-work for many of our placards.

This book is only a 'snapshot' of the work of the Coalition – many, in fact, most of the people whose activism has sustained the anti-war movement do not appear in any of the photographs here. We would want it to be otherwise but in a movement which, at its height, mobilised hundreds of thousands, this is not possible.

However, it is to those people that this book is dedicated. To those who wrote, spoke, agitated, booked the coaches, planned the meetings and made the banners – without you there would have been no Stop The War.

And finally we thank all those tens of millions who – across the world – marched on February 15th 2003. You were right and Tony Blair and George Bush were wrong.

We remember all those who have been killed in the 'war on terror'. The struggle goes on.

Andrew Burgin
Editorial Director
Press Officer of Stop The War

CREDITS

Banksy – Art
148, 149
www.banksy.co.uk

Chris Blake – Photography
185

Duncan Brown – Photography
169, 181
www.flickr.com/photos/duncanbrown

Kristian Buus – Photography
40-41, 54-55, 178
www.kristianbuus.com

James Cauty – Art
126, 127
www.l-13.org

Rudolf Cech – Photography
32-33, 196
www.rudcech.wordpress.com

Billy Childish – Art
143
www.billychildish.com

David Gentleman – Art
138, 139, 159, 161, 163, 164, 165, 172, 179, 180, 183,
185, 186, 192, 193, 195, 198

Richard Hamilton – Art
146, 147
www.infoloop.org

Dan Hancox – Words
www.dan-hancox.blogspot.com

Cliff Hanley – Photography
200

Clifford Harper – Art
132
www.agraphia.co.uk

Safa Kadhim – Photography
200
www.hadigallery.com

Karmarama – Art
125
www.karmarama.com

John Keane – Art
133
www.johnkeaneart.com

Richard Keith Wolff – Photography
44-45, 181, 189, 195
www.richardkeithwolff.co.uk

Peter Kennard – Art
120
www.peterkennard.com

Kennardphillipps – Art
118, 119, 121, 122,
www.kennardphillipps.com

Geoffrey King – Photography
23, 48-49, 189
www.geoffreykingphotography.com

Alan Kitching – Art
124
www.debutart.com

Leon Kuhn – Art
140, 141, 184
www.leonkuhn.org.uk

Mark Liebenberg – Photography
189
www.flickr.com/photos/mliebenberg

London Guantánamo Campaign
www.londonguantanamo.org.uk

Sue Longbottom – Photography
152

CND: Campaign for Nuclear Disarmament
MAB: Muslim Association of Britain
MFAW: Military Families Against the War
PSC: Palestine Solidarity Campaign
STW: Stop The War Coalition
TUC: Trades Union Congress